Wonderful Willy

by

Kathy Ansberry D'Aquila

Illustrated by

Diane Rogazione

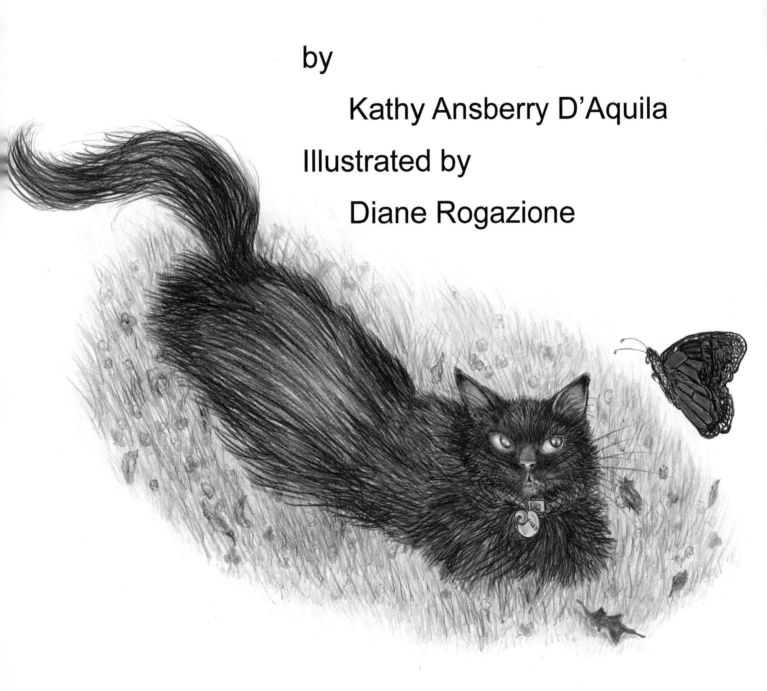

ISBN: 1479360996

ISBN 13: 9781479360994

Library of Congress Control Number: 2012917846

CreateSpace, Charleston, South Carolina

This book is dedicated to my husband, Dale
And to all my students at Cuyahoga Heights Elementary
School

Kathy

I would like to dedicate these drawings
To my wonderful parents

Diane

And of course, we dedicate this story
to our friend and inspiration:
Wonderful Willy

Kathy and Diane

Long black fur

1

Big green eyes

Chases bees

3

Eats dead flies

Teases his sister

Chases his tail

Crouches in the green grass

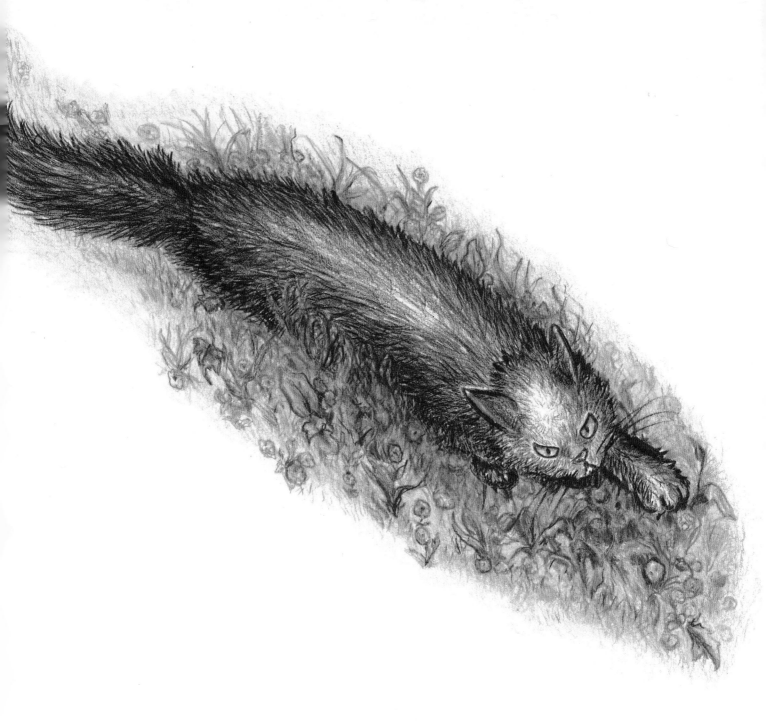

Opens our mail

Hunts little
chipmunks

9

Stalks a tasty mouse

10

"Leave it outside, Willy. Don't bring it in the house."

11

Leaps off the couch

12

Spins in circles
Upon the swivel chair

Spin him 'til he's dizzy.
He won't care.

14

Hold him in my arms
Like a baby sweet and mild

But Willy likes it upside down.
That's my wild and wooly child.

16

Perches way up high
Just like a jungle cat

17

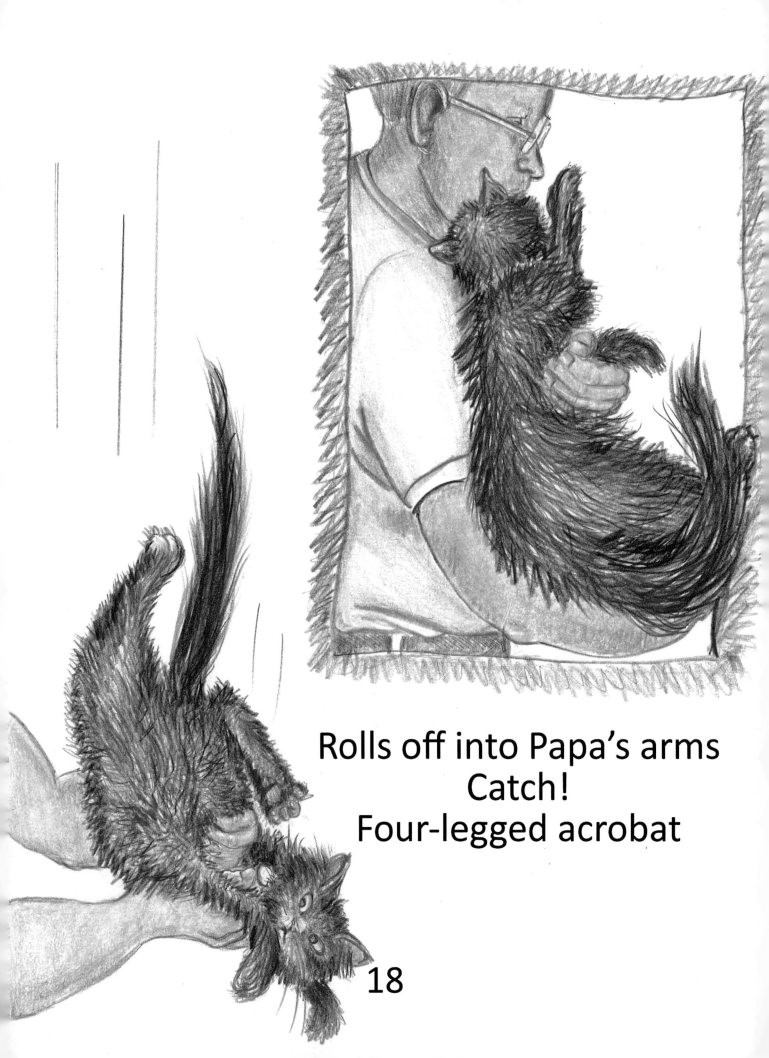

Rolls off into Papa's arms
Catch!
Four-legged acrobat

18

Had a real bad day?
Need a good long cry?
Willy will do tricks for you
until your tears run dry.

19

Jumps upon my desk
Drops into a heap
Chews papers, pens,
and pencils

And then he goes to sleep.

But when he gets
a little bored
or just plain tired
out,
he drops it in his
water bowl.
What's *that* all
about?

23

24

Wakes me in the morning
wet nose upon my face

"I love you, my sweet Willy.
No one can take your place."

About the Author

Kathy Ansberry D'Aquila has been an early childhood educator for 36 years and currently teaches first grade at Cuyahoga Heights Elementary School in Cuyahoga Heights, Ohio. She lives in Wickliffe with her husband, Dale, and four cats: Willy, Sofia, Annie, and Elmo. These lovable animal companions were all either strays or rescued from animal shelters.

About the Illustrator

Diane Rogazione often retreated to the safety of the local coffee shop to create her illustrations for *Wonderful Willy* since her own feline companions, Kitty Boy and Peach-a-nino, insisted on pouncing on the pencils and sitting on her drawings. ("Honestly, those cats have no respect for artwork!") Diane has been an educator for 31 years and comes from a long line of cat lovers. Her Aunt Eva has 22 cats!

Made in the USA
Charleston, SC
24 April 2014